# Spotlight on
# Peru

**Robin Johnson and Bobbie Kalman**

🍄 **Crabtree Publishing Company**

www.crabtreebooks.com

## Created by Bobbie Kalman

Dedicated by Robin Johnson
For Carmine and Laura, con amore

**Editor-in-Chief**
Bobbie Kalman

**Writing team**
Robin Johnson
Bobbie Kalman

**Editor**
Michael Hodge

**Photo research**
Robin Johnson
Crystal Sikkens

**Design**
Katherine Berti
Samantha Crabtree (cover)

**Production coordinator**
Katherine Berti

**Illustrations**
William Band: border, pages 18 (top left and right and bottom), 19, 20
Katherine Berti: pages 4, 5, 8, 18 (middle)
Bonna Rouse: page 17

**Photographs**
© Dreamstime.com: pages 14 (top), 25 (top left)
© iStockphoto.com: back cover, pages 8, 9 (top), 17 (top), 24 (top), 27 (top right), 28 (ceviche and corn), 31 (top)
© 2008 Jupiterimages Corporation: page 12 (top)
© Shutterstock.com: front cover, pages 1, 3, 4, 5, 6, 7, 9 (inset), 10, 11, 12 (bottom), 13, 14 (bottom), 15 (bottom), 16 (top), 17 (bottom), 19, 20-21, 22, 23, 24 (bottom), 25 (all except top left), 26, 27 (top left and bottom), 28 (potatoes and man), 29 (all except chili peppers), 30, 31 (bottom)
Other images by Comstock and Corel

**Library and Archives Canada Cataloguing in Publication**

Johnson, Robin (Robin R.)
    Spotlight on Peru / Robin Johnson & Bobbie Kalman.

(Spotlight on my country)
Includes index.
ISBN 978-0-7787-3456-7 (bound).--ISBN 978-0-7787-3482-6 (pbk.)

    1. Peru--Juvenile literature. I. Kalman, Bobbie, 1947-
II. Title. III. Series.

F3408.5.J64 2008          j985          C2008-901026-4

**Library of Congress Cataloging-in-Publication Data**

Johnson, Robin (Robin R.)
    Spotlight on Peru / Robin Johnson and Bobbie Kalman.
        p. cm. -- (Spotlight on my country)
    Includes index.
    ISBN-13: 978-0-7787-3456-7 (rlb)
    ISBN-10: 0-7787-3456-0 (rlb)
    ISBN-13: 978-0-7787-3482-6 (pb)
    ISBN-10: 0-7787-3482-X (pb)
    1. Peru--Juvenile literature. I. Kalman, Bobbie. II. Title.
F3408.5.J64 2008
985--dc22
                                              2008005109

## Crabtree Publishing Company

www.crabtreebooks.com          1-800-387-7650

Printed in the USA / 052017 / CG20170406

**Published in Canada**
**Crabtree Publishing**
616 Welland Ave.
St. Catharines, Ontario
L2M 5V6

**Published in the United States**
**Crabtree Publishing**
PMB 59051
350 Fifth Avenue, 59th Floor
New York, New York 10118

**Published in the United Kingdom**
**Crabtree Publishing**
Maritime House
Basin Road North, Hove
BN41 1WR

**Published in Australia**
**Crabtree Publishing**
3 Charles Street
Coburg North
VIC, 3058

# Contents

Welcome to Peru!                4

The people of Peru              6

Peru's land                    8

Plants and animals             10

Villages and farms             12

Peru's cities                  14

The government                 16

Early peoples                  18

The Inca Empire                20

Spanish rule                   22

Peru's culture                 24

Peru's art                     26

A taste of Peru                28

Explore Peru!                  30

Glossary and Index             32

# Welcome to Peru!

Peru is a small **country** in South America. A country is an area of land on which people live. It has **laws**, or rules, that its people must follow. A country also has **borders**, or imaginary lines that separate it from other countries. Peru shares its borders with five other countries. Find Peru and its neighbors on the map below.

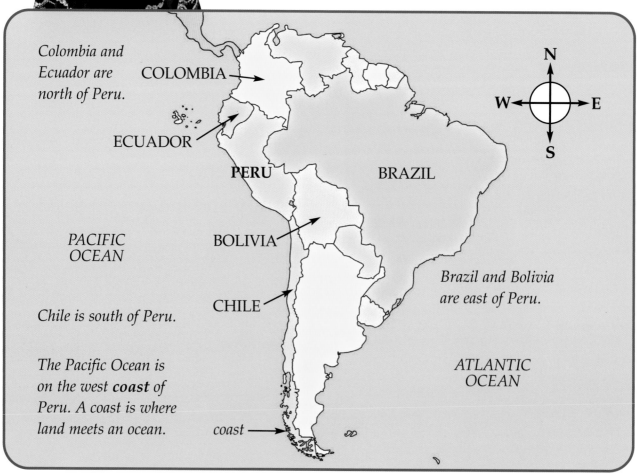

*Colombia and Ecuador are north of Peru.*

COLOMBIA

ECUADOR

**PERU**

BRAZIL

N

W — E

S

*PACIFIC OCEAN*

BOLIVIA

CHILE

*Chile is south of Peru.*

*Brazil and Bolivia are east of Peru.*

*The Pacific Ocean is on the west **coast** of Peru. A coast is where land meets an ocean.*

coast

*ATLANTIC OCEAN*

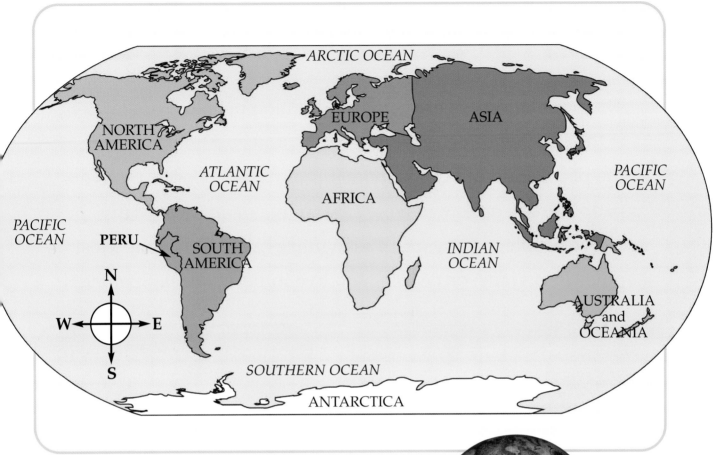

ARCTIC OCEAN

EUROPE

ASIA

NORTH
AMERICA

ATLANTIC
OCEAN

PACIFIC
OCEAN

AFRICA

PACIFIC
OCEAN

PERU

SOUTH
AMERICA

INDIAN
OCEAN

N

AUSTRALIA
and
OCEANIA

W E

S

SOUTHERN OCEAN

ANTARCTICA

## Peru, where are you?

Peru is located on the Pacific coast of South America. South America is a **continent**. A continent is a huge area of land. The other continents are North America, Europe, Asia, Africa, Australia and Oceania, and Antarctica. The seven continents are shown on the world map above.

5

# The people of Peru

The **population** of Peru is over 28 million people. Population is the number of people living in a country. About half of the population of Peru is made up of **native** people. Native people are people who were first to live in an area. Many native people in Peru speak a language called **Quechua**. Most other **Peruvians**, or people who live in Peru, speak Spanish.

*Many native people in Peru practice **traditional** ways. They wear the same style of clothing and make the same crafts as their **ancestors** did long ago.*

*Other Peruvians dress in today's styles and live modern lives.*

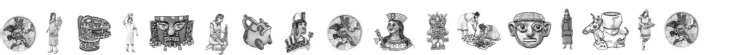

Some families in Peru have very little money. The children must quit school and work to help support their families. Other Peruvian families are wealthy. Their children go to **private schools**. They live in large homes and have comfortable lives. The girls in the picture below attend a private school in Peru.

*The people on these pages may look different, but they are all Peruvians!*

*There are many young Peruvians. Almost one-third of the people who live in Peru are under the age of 15!*

# Peru's land

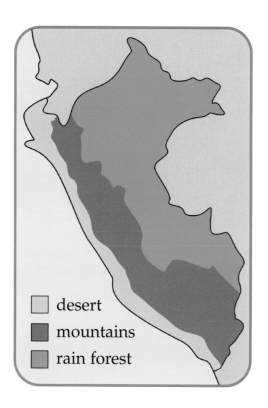

desert
mountains
rain forest

The Andes mountains lie in the middle of Peru. They divide the country into three **regions**, or areas. The mountain region is made up of hills, **valleys**, and grassy areas. The region west of the mountains is a **desert** area on the coast. The region east of the mountains is part of the Amazon **Rain Forest**. A rain forest is a thick forest that receives a lot of rain. The Amazon is the largest **tropical** rain forest in the world.

*Many people live in the **highlands** in Peru's mountain region. Highlands are areas of land that are on or around mountains. The **climate** in the highlands is mild. The land is good for farming.*

Most of Peru's people live along the coast. Peru's coast is **rugged**, or rough. It is also too dry for plants to grow. Rivers flow through some parts of the region, however. Plants grow well near the rivers because there is water under the ground.

This clown tree frog lives in the rain forest.

Peru's tropical rain forest covers more than half of the country, but very few people can live there. Rain forests have dangerous rivers and thick **vegetation**, or plant life. It is hard to travel from place to place. Many **species**, or types, of plants and animals live in the rain forest.

# Plants and animals

Different kinds of plants and animals live in the different regions of Peru. Many plants and animals live in the tropical rain forest. Others live in the mountain highlands or along the coast of the Pacific Ocean. The plants and animals of Peru are suited to their **habitats**, or the natural places where they live.

*Palm plants grow along the coast of Peru.*

## Life with llamas

Llamas are important animals in Peru. Ancient Andes peoples tamed llamas about 5,000 years ago. Since then, **highlanders** have used llamas to carry supplies to and from the mountains. They make clothing and blankets from the **fleece**, or wool, of the llamas and burn dry llama droppings for fuel. Highlanders also use llamas as a source of food.

Humboldt penguins build nests on the rocky coast of Peru. They swim in the Pacific Ocean.

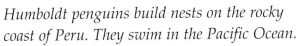

cacao pod

Cacao trees grow in Peru's rain forest. Their fruits are called **pods**. Cacao pods are used to make chocolate.

There are thousands of kinds of plants and animals in the Amazon Rain Forest. Many are **endangered**. Endangered plants and animals are in danger of dying out. This red uakari monkey is an endangered animal that lives in the Amazon Rain Forest.

**11**

# Villages and farms

There are thousands of **villages** in the countryside of Peru. Villages are small towns. Most villages are in the mountain highlands. A few native villages are found in Peru's rain forest. The rainforest villages are located along the edges of the Amazon and other rivers.

*This home is at the edge of the rain forest. It is on the Amazon River.*

*This village is on the island of Amantani. Amantani is in Lake Titicaca. People grow wheat, potatoes, and other plants on the hillside **terraces**. Terraces are flat, wide steps.*

Peruvian farmers grow potatoes, corn, tomatoes, bananas, coffee, and other **crops**. Crops are plants that are used by people. Most villages in Peru have markets. People sell the crops they have grown at the markets. They also sell clothing and **souvenirs**. Souvenirs are crafts that are sold to visitors.

# Peru's cities

Most Peruvians live in cities on the coast of the Pacific Ocean. The cities are busy and crowded with people. There are many houses, shops, and businesses. The biggest city in Peru is Lima, shown above. About one-third of Peru's population lives in and around this busy city. Lima is the **capital** of Peru.

*Iquitos is a city in Peru's rain forest. There are no roads to this city. Iquitos can be reached only by boat or plane.*

14

### The barrida

Many people move to Lima from highland villages and farms. They move to find better lives for their families, but there are not enough jobs in Lima. About a million people now live in a very poor part of Lima called the **barrida**. Houses in the barrida have no electricity or indoor plumbing. There are no schools or hospitals there.

*Most cities in Peru have **plazas**. A plaza is a public place where people meet. This beautiful plaza is in the city of Arequipa.*

# The government

*The flag of Peru has one white stripe between two red stripes. Some flags have Peru's **coat of arms** in the center. A coat of arms is a picture that stands for things that are important to the people of a country.*

The main **government** of Peru is located in Lima. A government is a group of people who are in charge of a country or part of a country. The government makes laws and important decisions for the people of a country. Peru's government is a **federal republic**. In a federal republic, the citizens of the country **elect**, or choose, their leaders.

*The **president** lives in the Government Palace. The president is the head of the government and the leader of the country. The Government Palace is in Lima, Peru's capital city.*

## Voting for the president

The people of Peru **vote** to elect their leaders. To vote is to choose one person from a list of people. Voting is **compulsory**, which means that people must vote. The people of Peru elect a new president every five years.

*Peru's flag with the coat of arms has been painted on the face of this child.*

### Peru's coat of arms

Peru's coat of arms is made up of several **symbols**. A symbol is a sign or picture that stands for something else. The vicuña stands for Peru's animals. It is the national animal of Peru. The cinchona tree stands for Peru's plants. The horn with coins spilling from it stands for the many **minerals**, such as copper, silver, and zinc, that are found in Peru.

 # Early peoples

People have lived in Peru for thousands of years. Early peoples learned math and **astronomy**, the study of the stars. They hunted and fished for food. They grew corn, potatoes, beans, squash, and other crops. The Chavin, Nazca, Moche, and Chimu were some of the first **civilizations** in Peru. A civilization is a group of people that shares languages, government, **religion**, and history.

## Old ways of farming

Some early peoples who lived in the desert built **aqueducts**. Aqueducts are pipes that carry water from one place to another. The people used aqueducts to bring water down from the mountains. The water allowed them to grow crops in the desert. People who lived in the Andes built and grew crops on terraces.

*Farmers have grown potatoes in the Andes for thousands of years.*

The Chimu people built huge cities. This picture shows the **ruins** of Chan Chan, the capital city of the Chimu civilization. Chan Chan was once a great city where many Chimu people lived.

The Chavin were one of the earliest civilizations in Peru. They created beautiful gold statues.

The Moche people were skilled at making and painting pottery. They **recorded**, or told about, their lives on the many pieces of beautiful pottery they made.

The Nazca people lived in the desert of Peru. They carved **geoglyphs** in the sand. Geoglyphs are huge shapes and lines that can be seen only from high above the ground. No one knows why the Nazca carved these pictures.

# The Inca Empire

The Inca was the largest and most powerful civilization in Peru. From 1438 to 1532, the Inca fought other civilizations and made its **empire** large. An empire is a group of peoples or countries that are ruled by one person or government. The Inca Empire controlled much of South America. It built great cities and ruled many people.

### The end of the Inca

In 1532, a Spanish explorer named Francisco Pizarro came to Peru. Pizarro wanted the riches and power of the Inca. He killed the **Sapa Inca** and thousands of his people. The Spanish later became the new leaders of the Inca Empire.

*The Sapa Inca was the ruler of the Inca Empire.*

The Inca created many beautiful works of art, such as these gold masks.

Machu Picchu is a very old Inca city built in the mountains of Peru. It is often called the "Lost City of the Incas."

# Spanish rule

The Spanish ruled Peru for over 300 years. During that time, they took control of the country's farms and **natural resources**. They forced the native people of Peru to work on the farms and in gold and silver **mines**. The workers were treated poorly. Many native people died in the mines. Many others died from new **diseases**, or illnesses, that the Spanish brought to Peru.

*Cusco was the capital of the Inca Empire. The Spanish destroyed Cusco and built a new city in its place. They built many new buildings on the **foundations** of old Inca buildings.*

## The fight for freedom

Most Peruvians did not want to be ruled by Spain. They wanted **independence**, or the freedom to rule themselves. In 1780, Túpac Amaru II led the Inca people in the first **rebellion** against Spain. A rebellion is a fight against a government. There were several rebellions in Peru. On July 28, 1821, Peru won independence from Spain. Each year on July 28, the people of Peru celebrate their freedom and their country.

*a Catholic church*

*Today, most Peruvians are **Catholics**, but many native people still practice their old religions. This cross shows both beliefs.*

23

# Peru's culture

Today, Peru's **culture** is a mix of Spanish and native ways. Culture is the beliefs, customs, and ways of life that are shared by a group of people. People **express**, or show, their culture through their art, music, dance, sports, clothing, and food. These pages show some of the ways that Peruvians express and celebrate their culture.

*The **zampoña**, or pan flute, is a very old Peruvian wind instrument. It is made of several pipes that are joined together. Each pipe is a different size and makes a different sound.*

*The **marinera** is a popular traditional dance. It is a graceful dance that is performed using handkerchiefs.*

The **charango** is the national instrument of Peru. This instrument is like a small guitar. It is often made from armadillo shells.

Peruvians love to play and watch *fútbol*, or soccer. It is Peru's national sport. Soccer was brought to Peru from Spain hundreds of years ago.

## Fiesta!

Peruvians celebrate their culture with **fiestas**. A fiesta is a party or a festival. During fiestas, there are parades, games, music, and dancing. People gather together to eat, drink, dance, and have fun! This Peruvian mask was made for a **Carnival** parade. Carnival is a celebration that takes place every February and lasts for several days.

25

# Peru's art

Art has been an important part of Peru's culture for thousands of years. Native Peruvians made useful and beautiful objects with the materials that were available to them. Many skilled craftspeople in Peru continue that **tradition** today. Some Peruvian artists and their crafts are shown on these pages.

*This native woman is **spinning** llama wool into yarn. To spin is to stretch and twist wool into strings of yarn. The yarn is used for knitting warm woolen hats, scarves, and sweaters.*

*After it is spun, the yarn is **dyed**, or colored. Name five colors that you see in the yarn above.*

*This woman is **weaving** yarn into cloth. The cloth will be used to make clothing and other items.*

Handmade Peruvian dolls are popular with **tourists**. A tourist is a person who travels to a place to learn about it and to have fun.

This artist is making pottery like the pottery made by the people of Peru who lived long ago.

*These colorful crafts are for sale at a market in Peru.*

# A taste of Peru

*Ceviche is a traditional Peruvian meal. It is made with pieces of cold fish, which are pickled in lemon juice. Ceviche is served with onions, sweet potatoes, and chili peppers.*

Food is another important part of Peru's culture. In ancient times, potatoes and **maize**, or corn, were the most important foods. People roasted potatoes or used them to make thick stews. They cooked and ate corn or used it to make bread and **tamales**. They also used corn to make **chicha**, or corn beer. Today, Peruvians combine these **staple** foods with other foods to create all kinds of tasty dishes.

*This Peruvian man is baking potatoes in a traditional oven.*

28

This woman is serving tea made from plant leaves.

Tamales are softened corn husks that are filled with meat or vegetables.

Chili peppers are used to flavor many dishes.

This Peruvian dish is called **causa limeña**. It is made with potatoes, eggs, and shrimp.

People who live near the ocean eat many kinds of fish. These fish were just caught.

# Explore Peru!

Each year, tourists from around the world visit Peru. If you were a tourist, what would you like to see? Walk through this doorway to discover some of Peru's wonders. Machu Picchu is just outside! Perhaps you want to take a hike. Wear comfortable shoes!

*You could hike the **Inca Trail** to Machu Picchu! The Inca Trail winds through the Andes mountains. The Inca built this road long ago. They used the road to carry goods and messages across the land. What messages would you send about this place? Write a story about your imaginary hike.*

blue morpho butterfly

The Amazon River is the second-longest river on Earth. It starts high in the Andes mountains and flows through the Amazon Rain Forest. You could take an **ecotour** to explore the river and the rain forest. You might see a beautiful blue morpho butterfly while you are there. What else might you see?

You could visit the Uros people, who live on Lake Titicaca. They live on small floating islands that they build from **reeds**. Reeds are tall woody grasses that grow in the lake. The Uros also use the reeds to make boats, homes, and furniture. The man on the boat is inviting you to go for a sail.

# Glossary

**Note**: Some boldfaced words are defined where they appear in the book.

**ancestor** A relative from long ago

**capital** The city in which a country's main government is located

**Catholic** A person who is a member of the Roman Catholic Church

**climate** The usual weather in an area

**crop** Plants grown by people for food and other uses

**desert** An area that receives very little rain

**ecotour** A tour to a natural place that teaches people about the environment

**foundation** The base on which a structure is built

**highlander** A person who lives in the highland region

**mine** A large area dug out in or under the ground, which contains minerals

**mineral** A non-living substance that is usually found inside rocks

**natural resource** Something found in nature that is useful or valuable to people

**private school** A school that charges money from its students

**Quechua** The language and name of a native group descended from the Inca

**religion** A set of shared beliefs about God or gods

**ruins** Buildings and other parts of a civilization that remain after the civilization has been destroyed

**staple** Describing a main food that is eaten every day, such as corn

**tradition** The passing down of customs and beliefs from long ago

**traditional** Describing ways that have been practiced for many years

**tropical** Describing a hot, wet climate

**valley** An area of low land between hills

**weave** To create a piece of cloth by joining strands of yarn or fabric

# Index

animals 9, 10-11, 17

cities 14-15, 16, 19, 20, 21, 22

civilizations 18-21

coasts 4, 5, 8, 9, 10, 11, 14

culture 24-25, 26, 28

desert 8, 18, 19

farming 8, 12, 13, 15, 18, 22

flag 16, 17

food 10, 18, 24, 28-29

government 16-17, 18, 20, 23

highlands 8, 10, 12, 15

Inca Empire 20-21, 22, 30

maps 4, 5, 8

mountains 8, 10, 12, 18, 21, 30, 31

native peoples 6, 12, 22, 23, 26

plants 9, 10-11, 12, 13, 17, 29

population 6, 14

rain forests 8, 9, 10, 11, 12, 14, 31

rivers 9, 12, 31

Spanish rule 20, 22-23

villages 12-13, 15